CONTENTS

Introduction

Some time ago, I resolved to make more of an effort to record my travels in the form of a visual *aide-memoire*. I've been fortunate in my textile teaching and have been invited to run classes in many countries, meeting some wonderful people, having some great experiences and taking lots of photographs.

In addition to the usual sketchbooks and albums, I began to keep personal stitched diaries, sticking inkjet-printed photos to a heavy cotton backing and adding a little stitch. It was a haphazard process, for my eyes only (and they were very prone to fading) but the idea evolved and grew into a series of work that I call my 'long diaries'. These combined quiet, fairly abstract areas – such as close-up images of rusty old boats or peeling paint – with photos of places, architectural features and people. Drawings, scraps of text and memorabilia were often included and these brought memories into very sharp focus. Luckily, the ink for today's printers is much more permanent. Mixed media techniques were also incorporated, adding extra texture and interest.

< *Long Diary* (80 × 38 cm, 32 × 15 in)
This was the first long diary I made. It records the adventures enjoyed on a variety of teaching trips, ranging from the heart of Wales to Australia, via Italy. The combination of photos and stitched pieces that were my teaching samples really brings back the memories.

The diaries are held together and decorated by hand or machine stitch and they're great for using up small pieces of stitching from your horde of samples – or what my friend Monica calls the 'failed experiments box'. When complete, certain areas of the long pieces often suggest individual works which stand alone, a spin-off from the diary. These days, the diaries are no longer just recordings of trips but have become a means of generating inspiration on many subjects. Apart from being artworks in themselves, they're used to explore ideas for further stitched pieces.

The diaries have recently evolved into pure fiction: textiles that tell stories. I can't tell you how much I've enjoyed making these as they seem to have a life of their own. Sometimes the tale that emerges has a completely different ending from the one planned.

In this book, I describe how I make and use my long diaries and tall tales and offer ideas and techniques for taking them further in many forms of stitch and mixed media.

∧ *Italian Sketchbook*
Keeping a sketchbook can be a great way to record your memories and use them to create a long diary. This one shows frescos and texture studies.

Wales to Wollongong

Before we get into the nitty-gritty of printouts and techniques, I want to use this section to describe how the components all work together. In the next section we will start from scratch and build up a Scandinavian version of a long diary, with detailed instructions for the techniques for stitch and embellishment.

It may be helpful to take a closer look at one of the original diaries. The one shown here follows our travels from the Italianate Welsh village of Portmeirion, through teaching trips to Puglia in Italy and Horsham in southern Australia. It even contains some class samples from the workshops. When you are gathering the material for your own piece, do think about the colour scheme and try to avoid sudden colour changes. Mine has splashes of bright colour but it is predominately green at the top, changing to blue gradually as it goes down. There are also a lot of neutral colours of grey and taupe. The diaries are intended to be quite 'busy' as I feel that this conveys the dynamic of travelling. This piece, in particular, reminds me that we covered these countries in a very short space of time and the movement through the countries conveys that to me.

You will note the photographs of places or people (or both) and it is these that most strongly bring back memories when looking at the diary later. However, too many photos are confusing to the eye and so it is necessary to bring in other elements that are related to the subject but are more abstract. For instance, in this diary I used a photograph of an old rusty pier which provided several restful areas for the eye. I also included photos of a stone carving, with quite neutral colours and some abstract subjects such as faded painted triangles on an old boat.

The next important part of the puzzle is a linking motif. This can be a strong shape and the repeat of this design will unite a piece of work. In my diary a carved stone worked well for this purpose. I liked the colour, which stood out without clashing with the other colours and also had some interesting detail in the form of circles. It was a great joy to find a very similar motif over a church door in Lecce, Italy, and these coincidences often happen if you keep your eyes open.

∨ A page from one of my travel journals. These differ from the sketchbooks in that they were made after returning home when a more considered approach could be taken. This one shows the rusty pier that featured in the *Long Diary* and some sample stitching.

> Attractive surface interest was created by the layering of the papers and the stitched pieces.

Crocodiles inhabit this area

Keep away from the water's edge a...

...xtreme care when launching

www.masse...

www.twisted...

A closer look

Let's look at the four main sections of this diary. In the photos, labelled 1–4 from top left, you can see how the integration works.

The header for this diary is made from a combination of two of my favourite materials: water-soluble paper and fine metal shim. I have used this technique in other books but a reminder of the details is shown in the next section, when we make a long diary from scratch.

The numbered points describe the materials and techniques that make up this long diary, a combination of scanned photos and pages from sketchbooks, stitched samples from the workshops taught and scraps of memorabilia.

1

The very top of the diary was formed from water-soluble paper on metal shim. Two of the stone carvings which form repeat motifs are shown here. This section also contains photos and prints taken from sketchbooks, with some simple hand stitching.

2

The next section moves from a 'mock-up' of Italy to the real thing and documents a teaching trip to the wonderful Masseria della Zingara in Puglia. In this section, scenes from the surrounding countryside, where we had outings to sketch, are combined with work that was prepared for the course. The two machine-embroidered landscapes were completed especially for the diary, as was the 'figures in the landscape' piece seen in the centre at the bottom of the picture. The column on the left of this section was added afterwards to balance the shapes and give a good edge.

In the penultimate section of this diary, further travels in Italy cover the historic city of Lecce where we discovered a lamp-post festooned with padlocks, a custom for local lovers to declare 'their love, locked in forever'. The boats in the harbour at Monopoli blended very well into the carving above. A statue of a learned gentleman provided a focal point here. He has been edged with satin stitch to proclaim his importance.

Finally, a whole new continent. Off to Australia and another teaching trip (it was a very active year) in Horsham in the west of Victoria state. At the top, the painted triangles from a boat were printed in strips to form a border between the continents. There is only one photo in this section as things were becoming rather busy. This picture brings back wonderful memories of the day when the tutors had a day off and were taken up a mountain to see eagles and to view wonderful aboriginal art. The remainder of this section is quiet, with photos of stitched stone carvings and a jetty with supports that provided colours of green and rust. With a little hand stitching, this photo, printed on normal printer paper and backed with felt, was turned sideways and made a good edging.

SECTION 2
Scandi Scribbles

The next long diary is based on a trip to Scandinavia, which offered some wonderful photographic opportunities. Having set out the basic concept in the previous chapter, it's time to look at methods and techniques for building up a diary from the very beginning. The photo on page 17 has been annotated to show where these techniques were employed in the finished piece. I'm not suggesting that you use similar subject matter or even the same techniques but the construction and selection of material will be similar for most of the diaries and tall stories in this book.

TECHNIQUES USED IN THIS SECTION

Many of the techniques covered here will be familiar to you. As some may be new, I have included them in more detail under the relevant headings below.

- Glossy photo paper
- Textured photos and prints on matt paper
- Printing on painted paper
- Easy drawing techniques
- Printing on Jacquard InkJetPrinting cotton and silk
- Cast water-soluble paper on metal shim
- Inchies

You'll find the details of materials and stockists inside the back cover.

Content

Start by gathering together your photos, paintings, printouts, stitched pieces, pages torn from tourist brochures, tickets or cards from museums and the odd print from a scanned sketchbook. An important thing to remember, for both matt and glossy prints, is to print on good photo paper as this makes an enormous difference to the result both in quality and fade resistance. It's not always the expensive stuff that's the best, so try a few if you can.

You need to find a design element or motif at an early stage, one that can be repeated several times to add unity to the finished piece. Remember the stone carving that appeared in the previous section? Bear in mind that too many disparate units confuse the eye, although good use of colour co-ordination can allow this rule to be broken.

> Sketchbook pages recording the old town in Stockholm. I print small photos straight from my camera and add quick on-site sketches.

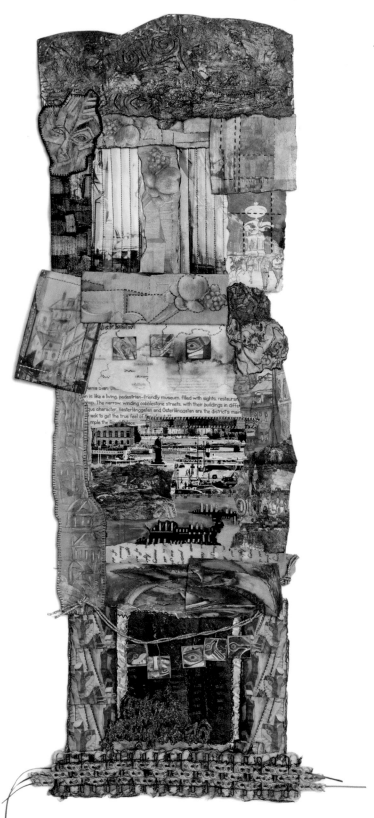

< A long diary Scandi style.
This diary combines
photographs with mixed
media work, stitched
pieces, maps and
mementos.

Photos

Now look for the location photographs, as these will give a sense of place. In this case four were chosen, two from Sweden and two from Denmark. One was printed on glossy paper while the rest were smaller, printed on matt, to give a contrast.

Motifs and patterns

Next, the accent motifs were selected. I used a stone carving, part of a wonderful metal column, some masks from a Stockholm window display, and a poppy I found at London's Gatwick Airport. The poppy colours were changed in a paint program on my computer but it would have worked equally well with the original photo.

Further elements were also made by converting photos of the masks into a repeat pattern, which is quite easy to do in a paint program.

Stitched samples

I found several pieces of stitching that fitted with the colour scheme and were about the right size. One was an experiment with stitched braids, threaded through paperclips. There was also a machine-stitched sample made from lettering, burned from poly cotton with a soldering iron. I added other pieces later, as the building of the panel dictated.

Techniques

a. Glossy photo paper

Try printing on glossy photo paper and then remove some of the black layer with a wet-wipe. This won't work with all printers as it depends on the ink but it's not vital, just interesting if you can get it to work. The photo was stitched to the centre of the craft Vilene background, using lines of straight stitch, with the foot on. Some machines don't like stitching on the shiny surface but, if you place your hands each side to help it along, it can usually be achieved with simple straight lines of stitch. If all else fails, work from the back, which throws up some interesting textures on the front.

∧ This photograph, of a view down a lane in the old town of Stockholm, was printed on glossy paper which was then partially wiped with a wet-wipe.

∨ Smooth prints can be a good foil to the crumpled ones, especially if a paint program is used. It can be very interesting to accent shapes with machine stitch and then work hand stitching through the machining.

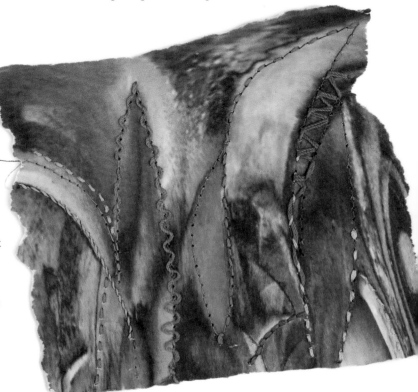

b. Matt photo paper

In many ways this can be much more useful than the glossy paper as it can be crumpled until soft. It can be used as a smooth surface as shown on this page. Always start with a clear print on good-quality paper that is not too heavy.

∨ This photo shows a pre-stitching technique where the sewing machine is used, with no thread, to make holes for hand stitching. This enables the paper to be bonded or glued to a firm backing.

> This pic shows how colouring the edge of the photo by running a marker along it will take care of any white edges.

∨ This stitched matt photo gives an idea of how coloured pencils can be used to give a 'hand-coloured' effect. It also shows how machine stitching with no thread can be a good way to enable hand stitching through thick backing fabrics.

For crumpled pieces use matt photo paper and add texture like this:

1. Gently crumple the paper, being careful not to tear it; it should be very creased and quite floppy. The image can be used at this stage, perhaps adding emphasis to some lines by drawing over them with pencil or pen after gently flattening the paper.

2. If you wish to add some oil, rub a little olive oil (most oils will work, so use what you have to hand) between your palms and then rub onto the paper. Hold up to the light to see how coated it is and repeat this step as necessary. Leave the paper for a day or two for the oil to absorb and then iron it gently, through baking paper, onto a backing. It will not be at all greasy and can be stitched by hand or machine.

Whichever method you use for the photos, check the colours at this stage. If there's a lot of white – such as buildings – try a gentle swipe with a wrung-out teabag. Sometimes this smudges or fades the colours, which is great if you then go over the lines with a pencil for a hand-drawn look.

Finally, back the photos by bonding them to Decovil (an 'iron-on' firm fabric) or use Bondaweb to iron them onto Vilene. Add simple stitching by hand or machine to decorate. It's not difficult to hand stitch through the backed paper, but use a strong needle and a robust thread and stick to simple running stitch or similar.

For paper bonded to thicker Vilene, try running the sewing machine, with no thread in it, around the shapes (use a slightly longer stitch length than usual) to make holes and then hand stitch through them. Buttonholed edges can work well, too.

c. Printing on painted paper

It's always interesting to print a photo or image on previously painted paper. It's usually necessary to reduce these pics to a black-and-white image. In most image manipulation programs, this colour reduction command is in the image menu. Reduce colours to two and then use the eraser tool to rub out any dense black areas. Don't worry too much about precision as the painted surface of the paper will obscure any mistakes. Use a heavy-weight paper so that it doesn't buckle and is flat enough for printing, and cut it to the size you would use for a letter – A4 in the UK. Paint using any media: watercolour, Brusho, Adirondack sprays. Any paint can be used, but don't make the colours too dark as too much saturated colour (such as a very deep, dark blue) will not show up the printed design. Try to blend the colours on the paper. Dry well, flattened under a weight (books are good) before printing.

Lettering can also be printed on pre-coloured paper, using either a suitable font or in your own handwriting.

> Here you can see how the poppy design was reproduced on crumpled paper and Jacquard InkJetPrinting cotton – see page 15. You can see a stitched version on the left of the photo. It also works well when the design is reduced on the computer to a black and white print. A great effect can be achieved when this is printed on previously painted paper, as you can see in the background.

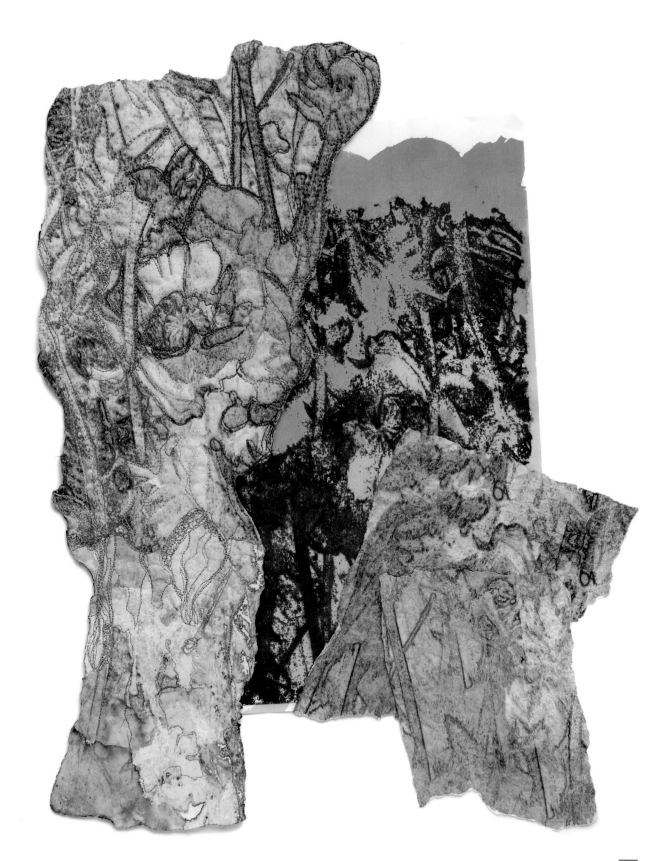

d. Easy drawing techniques

Method 1

All these printed photos and patterns can become a little 'mechanical' so I like to include some line drawings in my panels. I scan these in and then print them on pre-painted papers, cut to A4 (letter) size. Even if you think you can't draw, do have a go – or try the following:

1. Make more of the overprinted designs by printing the outlines in draft mode, and then drawing into them with a white pencil to highlight certain areas. The lines can be enhanced with a darker colour if this is needed. Then crumple them and add some stitching.

2. These can then be bonded or stuck to Vilene and stitched.

Method 2

Here is another idea for a drawing. I started with the photo of a window display in Stockholm which had some Cubist-style masks backed by bolts of interesting fabric. The original mask photo could have been used but it is always better to draw your own picture if you can and the Cubist theme was inspiring. Try this method:

1. Draw your own version of the Cubist mask by drawing rough outlines with a pen. It's fun drawing with a Cubist theme as the features have no need to balance and the whole thing can be as mad as you like. Make sure that the outlines are clear and that there are no holes.

2. Scan into the computer and then use a paint program and the bucket fill tool. Fill the closed areas with shades of grey. Keep the colours pale. Print on good-quality paper.

   or

   Use charcoal or soft pastel pencils to add light and dark areas to the outline. Work in shades of grey.

3. Now add colour with Coloursoft pencils, or similar. Colour over the top of the grey print or the drawing. This will give a computer design a 'hand-made' effect.

4. It is also possible to use the layers palette in a paint program to alter the image in many ways.

e. *Printing on Jacquard InkJetPrinting cotton and silk*

These Jacquard fabrics are available in cotton, silk or organza and I like the brand. Although the packs are not cheap, the fabrics, backed by paper, go through inkjet printers like a dream. They are also very stable with regard to lightfast qualities and they are washable, although this is of lesser concern for mixed media work.

Both the poppy and the larger of the stone-carved images were printed on Jacquard InkJetPrinting cotton. The poppy was free machine stitched onto felt and the stone carving was stretched over heavy-weight Vilene, after hand stitching. See above right.

The print-on silk was great for the repeat images of the masks and it was tacked to felt before being straight stitched by machine. This gave it a lightly quilted effect.

∨ Inkjet prints on Jacquard fabrics. The silk one was stitched and applied to fine metal shim to form the lower part of the *Scandi Scribbles Diary*.

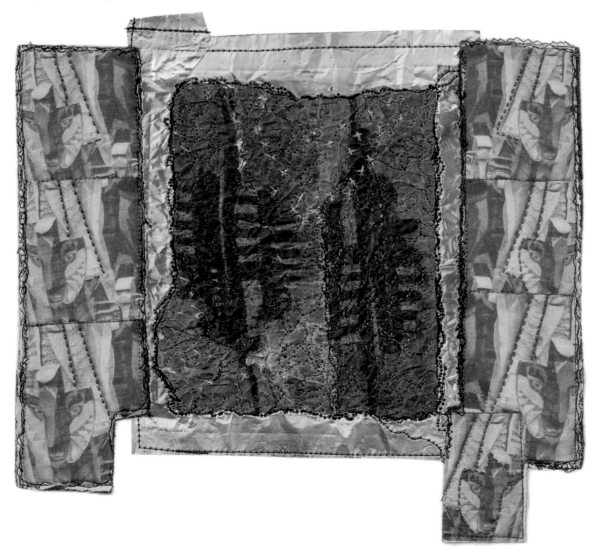

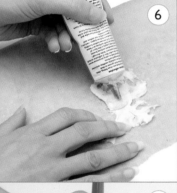

f. Cast water-soluble paper on metal shim

This technique is very good for making headers for diaries and panels. The first step is to make some cast paper shapes and water-soluble paper is ideal for this. Although it is not designed for paper moulding, it makes very precise and detailed casts when used as paper pulp. As long as it is well sealed when dry, it forms a permanent surface.

1. Use a rubber stamp or rubbing plate. Tear the paper into small pieces – stamp size is fine – and place them on the plate.

2. Now add some water with a paintbrush. Add the water slowly until the paper has turned to a mushy pulp.

3. Now move the pulp about with your finger so that you get some thin and holey areas. There will always be more pulp left than you expected so be quite ruthless.

4. Leave to dry in the sun or on a radiator. When it is dry, it will pop off the mould very easily.

5. Cut a rectangle of metal shim, slightly larger than the width of your panel. The height is up to you but allow a little extra to protrude around the top and the sides. This will be turned over the Vilene afterwards. Now stitch it to the Vilene, either with the normal sewing foot or free machining. Dissolve a little water-soluble on top of the metal.

6. Using a contact adhesive, place a small amount of glue on the back of the cast paper shapes to help the patterned water-soluble to bond to the metal. Stick pieces of the patterned cast paper between the pulp.

7. Merge them into the wet pulp areas with a damp brush.

8. When dry, use acrylic paint on the water-soluble paper (and on the metal as well if you like the effect).

9. A little gold paint, wax or pearly powder can be added when dry.

g. Inchies

Finally, there is the option of adding some small decorative details. These could be charms, beads, tassels or, as in this case, some inchies. Inchies are good-quality mountboard cut into inch-wide (2.5 cm) squares. Of course, it is possible to make your own but I find it helpful to have a packet of them ready when inspiration strikes, and they are not expensive.

We'll be looking at painting and embellishing them later in the book but, for this piece, they were simply vehicles for small squares of cut paper showing part of the mask drawing. These cut-outs were simply stuck on the inchie with PVA glue and the edges of the paper were trimmed afterwards. The sides were painted gold.

I also added them to a machine-wrapped cord (made by using your widest zigzag over string or yarn) and attached them to the cord, through a punched hole, by a string of small beads.

> *Scandi Scribbles Diary*, annotated to show where these techniques have been used.

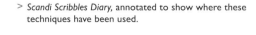

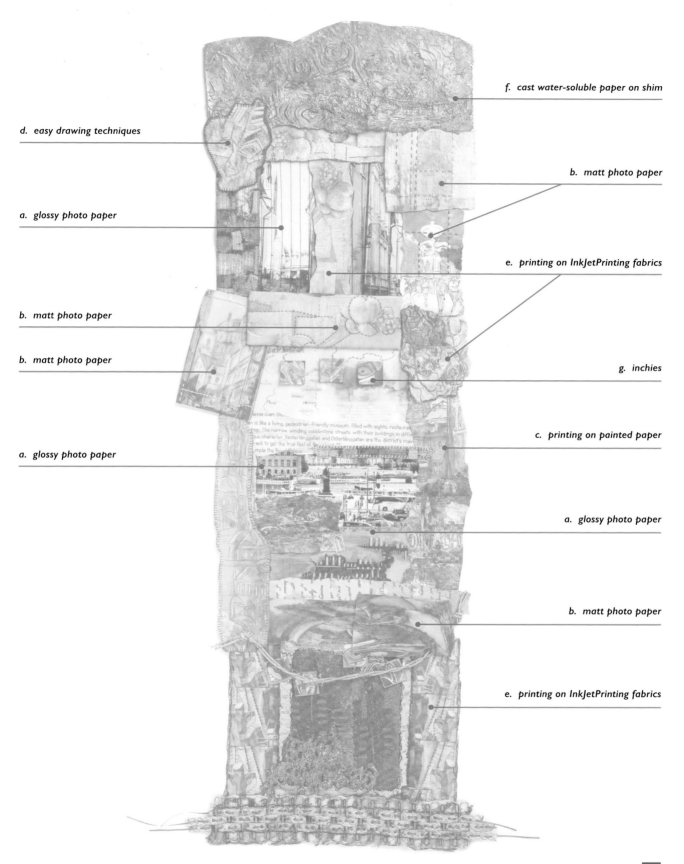

f. cast water-soluble paper on shim

d. easy drawing techniques

b. matt photo paper

a. glossy photo paper

e. printing on InkJetPrinting fabrics

b. matt photo paper

b. matt photo paper

g. inchies

c. printing on painted paper

a. glossy photo paper

a. glossy photo paper

b. matt photo paper

e. printing on InkJetPrinting fabrics

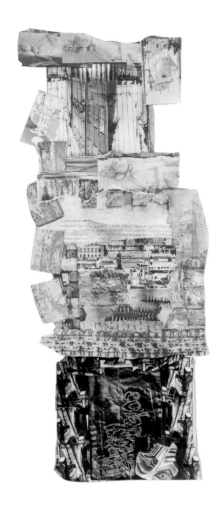

Rough trials

The components that look most useful can be printed in draft mode on cheap paper, then cut out and collaged on the reverse side of a roll of old wallpaper, just to get a feel for the composition. Carry the colours through as you go, trying for a subtle colour change or the introduction of a contrast colour that runs through two adjoining sections. When you feel reasonably happy with the design, take a photograph of it and print it out. This gives a better idea than just looking at the 'jigsaw' of pieces.

You can see some of the designs in this photo, combined with some scraps of stitching. These should be treated as a rough initial plan, as things change when you begin to stitch them together. In the final version, elements were taken from each of these designs. You can also work directly from your components if you like to take a more free approach.

Having decided on the components to be used in your sections, select the photos or images and print, crumple, wax, and back stitch them, as described earlier.

∧ Three rough designs for the Scandi diary. The components are much the same but the order varies. The one on the right is pretty close to the final panel. Don't feel that your design is cast in stone – go with the flow if a better idea occurs.

Making the hanging

Now it's time to put it all together and this is how I made mine. You may well develop your own way and that is fine. Be flexible and go with the flow if it all takes off in another direction. Here are some things to consider:

- Dividing the hanging into sections and working on these sections individually can be easier than struggling with a long and ungainly piece of work.

- Leave some backing Vilene at the top and the bottom of the middle section so it can be joined to the top and the bottom of the panel. Think about how this join will happen – can one area slide under another or will the join be covered by a stitched piece?
- Keep trying things as you go along, pinning the sections together if necessary. If the paper pieces are stitched, pin them in place on the Vilene through the stitching, or you will make too many extra holes.

The top of the panel

The top section of this diary was worked on a background of Vilene, roughly (36 x 28 cm, 14 x 11 in) – slightly larger than the expected finished size. A header was made from cast paper and shim and the edges were turned into the back of the Vilene.

The top of the panel is made from the following:
- a glossy photo with straight stitching
- two of the stone motifs
- a deliberately blurred photo of a noticeboard
- a photo on glossy paper with some colour removed and stitching added
- a piece of felt with applied silk from the oddments box
- the mask drawing.

The diagram on page 17 shows where the techniques described have been used. The pieces were pinned through the stitch holes to avoid making visible holes. When you are happy, stitch them down using a matching thread, either by hand with a strong needle, or on the sewing machine, in both cases securing the underneath pieces first. Don't forget to leave an empty space at the bottom to allow the middle section to join.

Eventually, the side edges of the craft Vilene will be trimmed close to the photo borders. However, for the time being, leave it as it is in case there's a change of mind.

The central section

The top section was a bit on the busy side so a simple area with not too much going on was needed to be a buffer at the beginning of this section. The colours also had to be considered as the materials gathered for this section had a green theme.

A map was scanned in for this section and printed in draft on matt paper. This makes it fairly pale and it works well combined with some lettering and a glossy photo of the Stockholm waterways. To complete this part of the middle section, another glossy photo of a metallic obelisk merged rather well. Further items in this area include the poppy, quilted onto felt, which was cut out and the edges were burned. Over-printed drawings, lettering and inchies were also used.

You can see here the effect produced by drawing method 1, from page 14. Printing an architectural feature in draft mode on painted paper provides a base for pencil drawing.

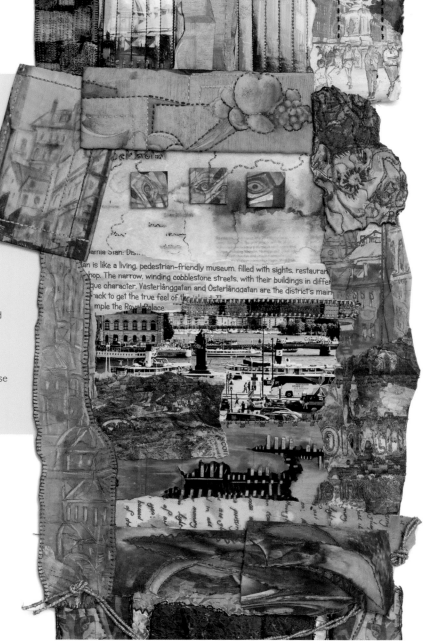

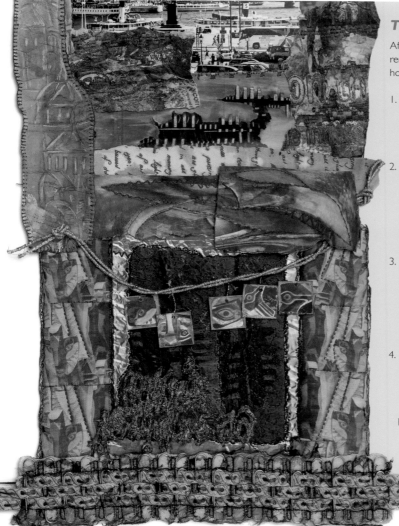

The bottom section

After cutting the Vilene for the background, the remaining prints were examined for possibilities. This is how the stitching went:

1. The design, showing the metal obelisk, was printed, crumpled and oiled. This piece was placed in the centre of the Vilene, leaving a wide border all around. It was secured to the background with free machine stitching.
2. Strips of metal shim, about an inch (2.5 cm) wide, were coloured, either by holding in a candle flame or by using a paint-stripping heat-tool (mind your fingers as it gets hot). Placed over the edges of the oiled paper, they were stitched to attach them to the background. More stitching followed, to cover the joins in the shim.
3. The photograph of the masks was made into a repeat pattern in a paint program and pasted in strips to form borders. Printed on silk, it was cut into strips which covered the edges of the shim. On top of the oiled paper, I stitched a machine-embroidered sample, by stab stitching (by hand) to the background.
4. The top of the shim border was covered by two smooth prints (matt paper not crumpled) in a toning design. Stab stitching was once again used to secure the pieces.

Finally, a heavy strip of stitching, comprising paperclips and woven strips, formed the bottom border. A dangly line of inchies, beaded to a machine-wrapped cord, was a great finishing touch.

Finishing

I'd like to say that it all went together in one go, exactly as described above but, in fact, a lot of time was spent in pinning it together, hanging it up and changing my mind.

Time to bring it all together, sliding the middle section into place and pinning any covering elements on top. Sew on a loop as a temporary hanging device. Now have a long hard look to see if it all works together. I often find that something needs to be taken away, or an extra component needs to be added, to balance shape or colour. When you are happy, stitch the sections together. They probably won't fit under the machine so this is best done by hand. I have been known to use a stapler as well to make sure it is really secure, but I only do this if it is an area with a covering element.

Any raw edges can be singed with a gas gun or candle, burning through the Vilene and the edging at the same time. Work outside or next to an open window and keep a damp cloth next to you in case it burns too well – in which case just wrap with the cloth.

< Stetchbook pages that inspired the panel shown opposite.

Extension techniques – diaries as inspiration

Stitched panel

It is possible to use the long diaries to generate designs for individual panels. I often take my L shapes (two pieces of mountboard cut into shape and used to isolate interesting areas of design) and look at areas of the completed work that could benefit from further investigation.

After careful thought and a little bit of jigsaw-like puzzling, the piece inspired by the diary concentrated on one area – Stockholm's old town (Gamla Stan). The view chosen was one that was used for the glossy picture in the top of the diary. The view was captured from a narrow alley in the oldest part of town, when I was playing 'looking through' games with the camera. Here I was looking through to the new areas of the town – although these were still pretty old by most people's terms.

Techniques used

The centre of the original image – the new town – was printed on good-quality, non-glossy paper which was then lightly oiled and crumpled. The main areas were highlighted with a drawing pen.

A drawing of the buildings in the alley was made on cartridge paper, taking particular note of the perspective. This could have been a printout but the simplified pen drawing proved a better choice for leading the eye into the central area.

Further prints of the old town were scanned and enlarged, changed to greyscale and dabbed with tea. They were torn out, placed on felt and buttonholed around the edge.

The 'displaced' poppies (an oiled paper print) inject a shot of colour. They were made, as for the main panel, using the paint program's 'Displacement Map'.

The bottom of the work is a strip of the same displaced poppy printout but this time it is just crumpled – not oiled. This machine-stitched strip is enhanced by a brilliant find from the 'bits box', a stitched cut-out design of machined rectangles and wrapped circular paperclips.

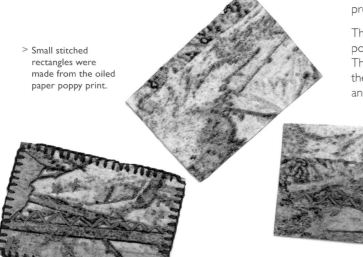

> Small stitched rectangles were made from the oiled paper poppy print.

Final touches were some small rectangles of oiled paper, again from the poppy design, with hand stitching. Some lettering, stitched using a sewing machine's lettering function, was added in order to 'explain' the piece.

> *Scandi Sketches*
  (46.5 x 23 cm, 18 x
  9 in). The 'looking
  through' section from
  the sketchbook was
  produced on crumpled
  paper and some areas
  were enhanced with
  a pen. Oiled paper,
  cartridge paper and a
  stitched zigzag piece
  were combined in
  this spin-off from the
  long diary.

Cotswold Memories by Nina Humphreys

I'm going to hand the beginning of this section over to Cornish artist Nina Humphreys, whose work I have long admired. When I saw her latest piece, her work chimed so well with the concept of the long diary that I simply had to include it in the book. It took the form of a visual diary based on a Summer School with Shelley Rhodes, run by Siân Martin's Distant Stitch School (www. distantstitch.co.uk). Using leaves, twigs, fir cones and other natural objects as source material, decorative surfaces were produced as a single large piece of paper-like material. Nina then used this to construct the finished items at home in her studio.

The main body of the work comprises recycled paper, gesso and gelli-plate printing techniques using a variety of papers and fabrics. The colours are soft and relate perfectly to the subject matter. In this section we won't pass on any details of the techniques used, as that would be unfair to the tutor, but we will look at the construction. Any of the techniques in the previous section would work well here.

< *Woodland Walks*
(33 x 26 cm, 13 x 10 in)
The 12 squares have been cut from the large piece of painted paper. The squares were machined into place with a machine-cord tree trunk outline and free machining was worked over the surface. Small 'bundles' of grasses, twigs and leaves were wrapped in cloth and applied onto the panel. Handwoven picot 'leaves' are worked to represent leaves and ferns. Twigs were painted and then wrapped with fine threads as a finishing touch and a focal point to draw the piece together.

> *Clutch bag*
The initial piece of paper-like material was extremely useful, and has been used in all of these projects. There was a large piece left, so Nina made a small clutch-bag, just the right size to store some art cards.

∨ *Fern Inspirations*
(29 x 26 cm, 11½ x 10 in)
This piece was constructed from a series of Gelli-plate
prints. Layers of acrylic paint have created an almost
fossilised effect.

< *Woodland Walks*
(94 × 26 cm, 40 × 10 in)
This is a hanging that
takes ferns as its main
design theme. It was
constructed using some
gelli-printed fabrics and
decorated paper, cut
from the large sheet.
Some real ferns were
added, sandwiched
between tissue paper
and sheer fabrics.

> *Woodland Frames*
(57 × 15 cm, 22½ × 6 in)
This is a smaller hanging
using up all the bits. Nina
gave herself a challenge:
to use all the paper and
fabric that was made at
Summer School, which
meant that this final
construction was made
from smaller pieces.
These were initially
pinned onto a silk
organza background
but, as things developed,
they ended up being
cut and rearranged
many times before she
was satisfied with the
overall shape. Eventually,
dyed fabric was added
which created the frayed
edges to the work. The
resulting small elements
fitted well together and
were then linked with a
machine-made cord.

< These sketchbooks show the hasty church
window sketch and two alternative landscapes.

Altered landscape

After our trip to the Cotswolds
with Nina, it's back to me and
recollections of a trip to Wales.
This shorter variation on a long
diary focuses on one or two
rough landscape drawings produced
during a short holiday there. On the same
break, a wonderful stained-glass window was
discovered – an abstract landscape in rich shades
of blue. The church was closing, so a quick sketch
was all that could be managed.

TECHNIQUES USED IN THIS SECTION

- Computer design (optional)
- Embellisher machine ideas
- InkAID on lace
- Pebeo Prisme medium
- Gesso on paper
- Lashings

*The following account of the making
of this piece includes some computer
design techniques but, if you don't 'do'
computer design, bear in mind that it
would work equally well with photos or
simple silk and acrylic painting on paper
or fabric. Just follow the suggestions for
varying the colour and fabric.*

On my return home, I scanned one of my landscape drawings and the stained-glass sketch into PaintShop Pro and used a variety of colour manipulations and the 'clone' tool to combine the two designs to produce an 'altered landscape'.

Some of the design techniques used can be found on the d4daisy website (www.d4daisy.com) in the section for this book, but I'm sure you have your own favourites. I took sections of the altered landscape design and rearranged them to form strips which were then printed. The stained-glass effect was enhanced by thickening some of the lines. This final image was printed twice on good-quality paper and was then crumpled and bonded to a large piece of craft Vilene to form a background. Very little of this can be seen in the final design but it's always good to get a base of colour down quickly.

Stitched pieces

The next step was to find my stitched pieces from the experiments box. I found two small samples based on trees, together with a stitched apple (product of a tree). A tree theme was emerging.

- A tree design which had been free machined on a background of white felt, overlaid with coloured silk fibres and topped with a chiffon scarf, before being lightly zapped with a heat gun. It was a little pale so I used the embellisher machine and a small piece of black chiffon to work over the top and tone it down a little.
- A birch tree which had been printed on crumpled paper and quilted onto felt, as described in the previous section.
- A stitched apple, made by using the embellishing machine on felt with wool fibre. Hand stitching added extra interest. This was then surrounded by a heavily machine-stitched background.
- A piece of lace which had been computer printed using inkAid (more on this technique on page 37).

∨ The stitched pieces that formed part of the panel. From left to right: a piece of inkjet-printed lace that had been coated with inkAID, a crumpled paper birch tree, an embellished and stitched tree and a wool-embellisher apple.

Dark-dappled wood, your secret keep.

Bright apples shining in the deep.

It did seem that a tree theme was being forced on me, which was appropriate as we had visited a wonderfully tree-mangled place called Puzzlewood, where we had a picnic. Appropriately, we ate apples. I hit on the idea of setting the tree and apple pieces within the stained-glass landscape. Thanks to the black lines of the stained glass, my landscape design resembled strips, so a diary composed of strips, woven over a background, seemed the way to go.

Samples of the stained-glass design were printed on a variety of papers and fabrics, using the following for the cut-out strips:

1. Original design printed on good-quality printing paper before being crumpled.

2. Original design printed on a sheet of Jacquard InkJetPrinting cotton and then bonded to felt before being distressed using the embellisher machine.

3. Original design given added vibrancy by printing on good-quality paper and then colouring some of the paler sections with markers. These act like paint but don't make the paper quite so wet (and are not nearly so messy).

4. Printed cotton bonded to felt – as before. This sample had a black chiffon scarf embellished on top.

> This is the background for the panel with 'experiments box' pieces in place. At this stage, it was in one piece.

Putting the piece together

The first idea was simply to weave the printed strips, leaving gaps for the stitched items within the weave. However, this looked rather boring so the following steps were taken to make the strips more interesting.

1. The strips were cut into different lengths and widths.

2. The Jacquard InkJetPrinting cotton strips were applied to black felt using an embellisher machine. One of these was enhanced further with a black chiffon scarf embellished over the top. These strips were edged with satin stitch.

3. The birch tree image was printed on glossy photo paper to give surface interest.

4. Printing the design on overhead projector transparencies gave added depth when placed over the same printed design.

At this point I decided that there was just too much material for one panel and it would work well as two smaller ones. The original background was cut in two and the next attempt at arranging all the strips on top gave much better results.

Now it was time to add the horizontal and vertical strips over the two backgrounds. One of the pieces went together very quickly. All it needed was a little poem, printed on tea-stained paper, to reflect that weird apple in a weird wood. One of the crumpled paper panels was hand-stitched with lots of seeding stitches to provide detail.

> Altered Landscape
> (32 x 22 cm, 13 x 9 in)
> Small pieces of stitching were enhanced by strips of hand stitched landscape on crumpled paper.

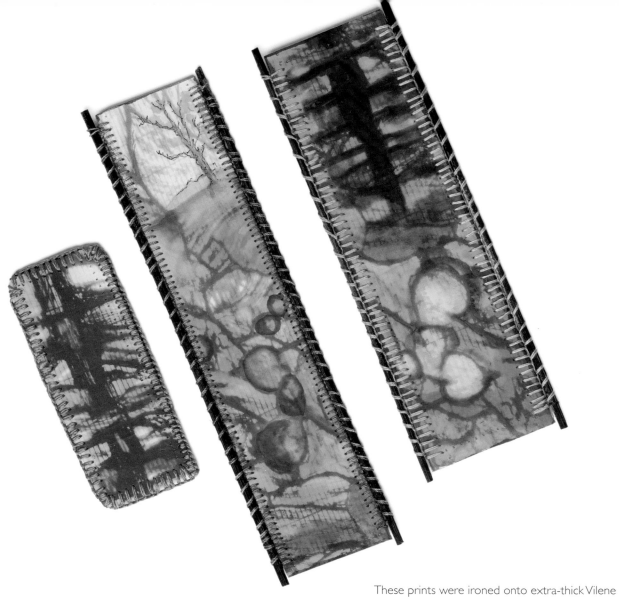

∧ These lashed, hand-
coloured sections form
focal points and raise
the surface a little.

Focal points

The other piece needed more surface
interest so I went in search of a focal point
in the form of a raised surface. Three narrow
rectangles of the design were selected and
printed on good-quality paper. Additional
drawing with a marker was added to provide
more contrast and the colour of the stones
was changed to turn them into apples to
match the stitched apples.

These prints were ironed onto extra-thick Vilene
S133 and, after making the holes with the sewing
machine, they were edged with buttonhole stitch
by hand. Finally, they were 'lashed' to painted
kebab sticks to give a defined edge. I mounted
them on three inchies, stacked and glued
together to raise them, before sticking them in
place on the piece.

This is quite a busy piece in a different format
from the previous diaries. It is a bright and
colourful way to bring back the memory of a
good holiday.

> *Altered Landscape 2* with lashed details applied on top.
(32 x 22 cm, 13 x 9 in)

Extension techniques – landscapes as inspiration

As before, it was possible to see how the landscape piece could be examined as a source for other work. In this case it was the tree studies that inspired.

Crumpled paper

I loved the pale stems of the birch trees that the computer design experiments had produced. These were printed in various sizes on good-quality coated paper and then prepared like this:

1. Crumple and oil the paper, as before.

2. Tear the edges and apply a light coating of Spraymount to the back.

3. Place on commercial felt, cut slightly larger than the paper and press it down onto the felt. Don't lose all the crumples when pressing.

4. Leave it for a day or two to let the stickiness wear off.

5. Stitch by hand or machine, as you prefer – or try a mix of each.

⩽ A birch tree was printed on oiled
⩾ paper and hand and machine stitched.
The photos, on the right, show the
original design and the manipulated
design. The final printed piece, ready
for stitching, is shown left.

(1)

(2)

(3)

(5)

(6)

(8)

∧ Printed and gesso-painted 'sliding techniques' cards.

Sliding gesso trees

As Christmas was approaching, I felt that the wintry birch design would be ideal for Christmas cards. These demand a less intense approach so I ditched the stitch and found a very simple and effective way of making the cards. You'll need some card blanks and a little pot of gesso. Work like this:

1. Batch-print the tree design on good-quality paper, making it slightly smaller than your card blanks. You can use the same design or a variety.

2. Crumple the paper but do not oil it.

3. Carefully tear out each individual design.

4. Lay it over the card and work out where it will be stuck. Then allow a border around it as it will be smaller when the paper is applied. Mark the corners with a pencil.

5. Cover this area with glue from a glue stick.

6. Place the paper on top of the glue and gently slide it in place, using your fingers to push the paper around the trunks to make them protrude slightly.

7. Add any extra glue around the edges, if required.

8. Leave for a day and then, very lightly, use a small brush to apply gesso as a highlight for the trunks and perhaps around the base vegetation. Don't overdo it – think 'dry brush' technique and add layers rather than a splodge.

Gesso can also be used for landscape studies. The small concertina book below, was made by applying gesso to smooth paper with a palette knife. While it was wet, it was sprayed with black Quink (fountain pen) ink which dries to beautiful blue-grey shades. A little coloured pencil work was added when it was all dry.

∨ Blue-grey gesso landscape.

InkAID

This is a thick fluid which coats paper before printing to give results that enhance clarity and colour. It is useful on its own, perhaps painted on cartridge paper, when a thicker paper is needed. Very fine papers, such as Japanese tissue paper, can also be stuck to ordinary printer paper and coated.

However, it can also be painted over collages of fine fabrics – such as scrim or flat lace (stick these to paper first), as in the 'experiments box' sample on page 29, which was inkjet-printed on lace. Please note that you need a simple printer of the 'in at the back, out at the front' style –and we do suggest that you use an old printer for these experiments. We take no responsibility for your printer but I would just say that I have been using this method for years and haven't had any problems. I now keep a cheap printer especially for inkAID as I use it a lot.

Work like this:

1. Take a piece of paper of a good weight and coat it with inkAID. The matt version is a good all-rounder.

2. Add pieces of pale-coloured scrim or fine lace – nothing too bulky. Paint more inkAID on top.

3. When quite dry, iron them very flat and then print, using the 'best photo quality' setting for your printer.

4. Use the result with the paper backing included – don't peel it off.

An alternative to paper is to apply fine lace to Jacquard InkJetPrinting paper-backed cotton. Use inkAID to apply it to the paper and then give another light coating on top of the lace.

> Lace and scrim were applied, using inkAID, to InkJetPrinting cotton. This gave a fabulous texture.

SECTION 4
Tall Tales

This part of the book was intended to be loosely based on the theme of fantasy. However, some time ago I became inspired by a book entitled *Mythago Wood* by Robert Holdstock which is based on an actual place in Kent. In the stories, Ryhope Wood is an ancient woodland which appears on maps as no more than three square miles in area. The wood is much, much bigger on the inside than on the outside and is inhabited by Mythagos – mythical images in human form – which have evolved from the imagination of men and the telling of tales. King Arthur, Robin Hood, the Green Man – they are all there, fighting, falling in love and generally causing mayhem. It's a bit like 'Lord of the Rings meets Harry Potter' and a good read if you like that kind of thing.

TECHNIQUES USED IN THIS SECTION

- Jacquard InkJetPrinting silk
- Matt photo paper
- Water-soluble paper
- Pressure stencils
- Printed Evolon
- InkAID
- Texture gels and stencils
- Pebeo Prisme on twinchies

Having read several of the *Mythago Wood* books, I started a sketchbook based on this magical place and thought it might provide inspiration for a panel. It certainly did that and gave me several characters for my story, including the Maiden and the Wise Woman.

> The cover of the Mythago Sketchbook showing one of the Wood Warriors.

> *Peace-seeking in the Land of Myth and Legend* (80 × 30 cm, 32 × 12 in) This panel depicts a tall tale about a band of heroes seeking Peace Island. Techniques include the use of Pebeo Prisme paint effects, pressure stencils, texture gels and a variety of inkjet printing methods. The story is told through bands of text.

A hero was required and my friend Jane obliged by letting me use one of her paintings. She is a wonderful artist and this painting of a very colourful character was just what was needed. One of my stitched icon pieces volunteered herself for the job of Wise Woman, and a drawing of a maiden from my myths sketchbook gave me my full complement of characters for the first panel. You can see the originals on this page.

These three characters were photographed and printed on Jacquard InkJetPrinting cotton and then ironed onto Decovil. When they had been cut to shape, I added a little stitch and buttonholed the edges. Further characters joined the crew at a later stage.

∧ *The Wise Woman.*
   Heavy stitch on felt with additional applied fabrics

< *The Hero*, by Jane Wild.
   Oil pastel on card

> *The Maiden.*
   Drawing pencils on paper with stitched leaves

The Maiden and the Peace~Seeker set out on the quest to find Peace. They have been told by the Wise-Woman that this is a land beyond the wild wood.

They use a Questor-engine (similar to Google) to find a map.

The Maiden and the Peace~Seeker set out on the quest to find Peace. They have been told by the wise-woman that this is a land beyond the wild wood.

∧ Calligraphy used to tell short sections of the tale.

While I was dithering about a plot, the hero named himself the 'Peace Seeker' and demanded a map, so that he could lead the others in the search for Peace Island.

When working on a narrative textile, it is essential to find a way to tell the story. In this piece, there are two areas of text that give a short version of the tale. My husband had to learn basic calligraphy at school so he is very useful at times like this. He wrote the text in black ink and I scanned it in and changed the colour to give an aged look. This text could easily be created using a suitable font in a paint program.

So now I had the cast and the beginnings of the story, which just left the making process for the start of their adventures.

Making the panel

I had been thinking in terms of a book of their quest but felt the need to make a 'long hanging' first as it is such a good way to try techniques and bring thoughts together. A narrow panel, mounted on a canvas stretcher (the type designed for acrylic paintings), seemed a good start. This is a tried and tested approach for me as I dislike mounting textiles behind glass – and I knew this would work.

A piece of craft Vilene was cut slightly smaller than the stretcher, after which felt, cut to the same size, was stitched to the Vilene. This formed the backing for a variety of smaller pieces. I describe here the techniques used for the textile, working down from the top of the panel. Many of the methods are covered in greater detail earlier in the book.

You can see the finished 'Peace Seeker' panel opposite. The letters correspond with the techniques described in this section.

a. Pebeo Prisme paints

The header bar was made from painted paper, crumpled and stuck to a strip of card that is 2 in (5 cm) wide. Thin strips of mountboard (or thick card) were cut and painted before being used to edge the painted segment. The sides of the strips were painted too. I then used twinchies (2 in inchies), and Pebeo Prisme to make elaborate tiles. I worked like this for the twinchies:

1. Paint a coat of PVA glue over the card squares and allow to dry.

2. Edge them with a thin line of Pebeo Cerne relief paste. This contains the Prisme fluid within the shape.

3. Use a kebab stick to give the Prisme fluid a good stir. Then collect a generous dollop on the end of the stick and drop it in the centre of the square. You may have to do this a couple of times. Tilt the square so that the liquid runs to the corners – you can help it by giving it a nudge here and there.

4. Add another colour if you wish, using a new kebab stick and stirring it into the existing colour.

5. When almost dry, tilt slightly to allow the colours to blend and the pattern to elongate. You could leave this propped against something like a lid to dry.

When quite dry, the squares were glued to the strip. I made four, which suited the size of my panel. I did have to glue them to the top of the panel, so leave room when you construct the next section.

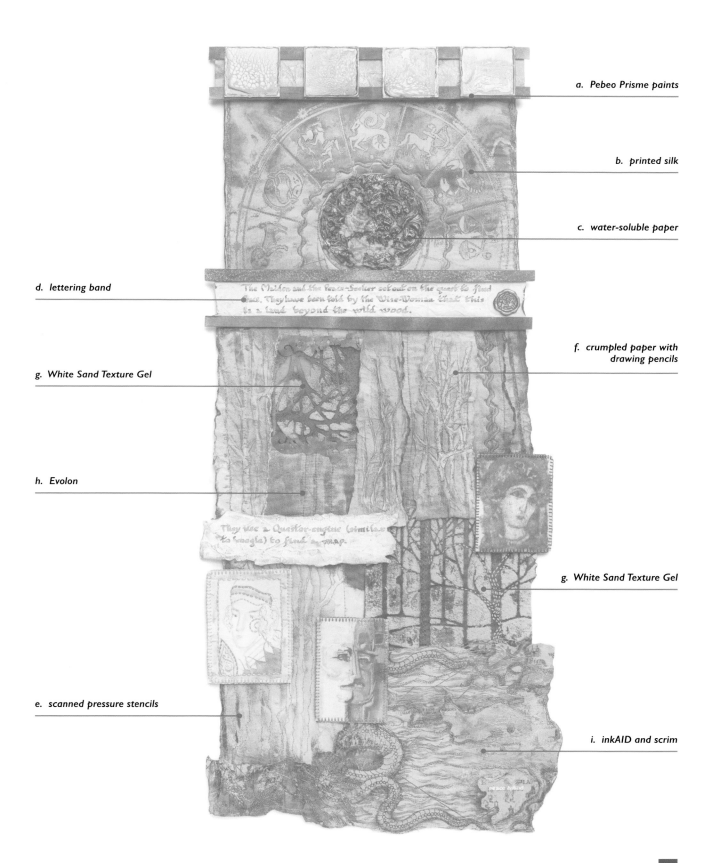

a. *Pebeo Prisme paints*

b. *printed silk*

c. *water-soluble paper*

d. *lettering band*

f. *crumpled paper with drawing pencils*

g. *White Sand Texture Gel*

h. *Evolon*

g. *White Sand Texture Gel*

e. *scanned pressure stencils*

i. *inkAID and scrim*

b. Printed silk

Something mystical was called for, at the top of the panel. I considered astrological signs, and a quick web search produced inspiration. Google images had some good copyright-free designs but, in the end, I produced my own work, using PaintShop Pro to meld together geometric shapes in the form of a divided semi-circle, with a colour-washed background. I printed it on paper and drew in some birth signs before scanning the whole thing again and printing it on Jacquard InkJetPrinting silk. The silk was sprayed with 505 Spray, a temporary adhesive, and placed on the felt/Vilene backing, 2 in (5 cm) from the top. It was then tacked before being stitched along the design lines, using the normal sewing foot, feed dogs up. The felt underneath gave a quilted effect.

The header needed a central boss so a circle was drawn, near the base of the header, to resemble something like a compass – a golden compass of course (I know my Philip Pullman). This was filled with painted water-soluble paper, as for the panel headers in the earlier sections. Here's the technique.

v The top of the panel was made from printed silk, lightly quilted, with a water-soluble paper 'boss' in the centre. A narrow band of lettering begins to tell the story. You can see detailed instructions for making the water-soluble paper boss and the lettering band on the next page.

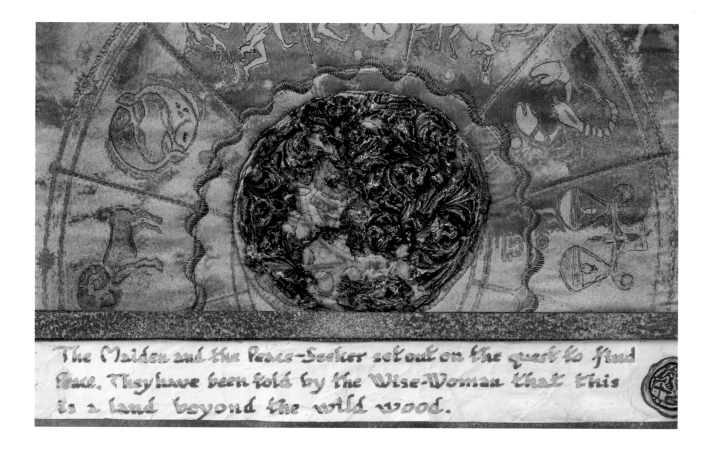

c. Water-soluble paper

Moulded paper came to mind when considering techniques for the boss. I had just the thing to use as a mould – a pot pourri lid. Although it's not designed for paper moulding, the fact that water-soluble paper is intended to dissolve means that its composition is such that it makes very precise and detailed mouldings when used as paper pulp. As long as it is well sealed when dry, it forms a good permanent surface.

1. Small pieces of the paper were placed on the lid and water was added sparingly, with a paintbrush. This mix was pushed into the shape as it dissolved, leaving some areas uncovered.

2. When dry, it was eased from the lid by pushing upwards from underneath, through the holes (don't worry if bits break off, it's supposed to look battered). It was turned inside out so the pattern was on top.

3. It was then painted with burnt umber and dark blue acrylic paint to seal it.

4. Finally, when the paint was dry, gold wax was applied.

5. It was left for a couple of days before being carefully stitched into place.

d. Lettering band

Moving on down the panel, it became obvious that some means of telling the story had to be incorporated into it so I wrote the beginning, as it had been told to me by the Peace Seeker. My long-suffering husband then transcribed it, using italic pens, only to see me scan it into a paint program and fade some parts out. After all, a good story needs a mysterious manuscript which has to be carefully deciphered. If you don't have access to a calligraphic man, the lettering could easily be made using a Word font in a large size and a brownish colour. Or try the fonts in your paint program.

The wording was printed on tea-stained paper and stuck to a strip of card. Thin strips of mountboard (or thick card) were cut and painted before being used to edge the lettering segment. Paint the sides of the strips too. Finally a little plastic charm (actually a seal from the top of our brie cheese boxes, painted gold) was glued in place. The lettering piece was not secured to the background immediately as it needed to sit on top of the join between the top and the middle of the panel.

The remainder of the panel was worked in the following way, stitching the components to the base fabric along the length of the panel.

^ This silk was patterned
with a pressure stencil.

e. Scanned pressure stencils

Now the adventure could begin and it was pretty obvious that it all had to start with the wood. I'd already tried several ways of portraying this when putting the initial sketchbook together and found that commercial stencils of woodland trees (made by Clarity; see Suppliers) gave good results with a variety of methods and materials.

Forming stencils by pressure is an easy technique which gives great results for fantasy forests. Just lay the plastic stencils on wet painted paper or silk and hold them in contact with the substrate by placing the odd bottle, or similarly weighted object, on top. This gives a misty, diffused image which suited the subject well. A piece of silk, treated like this, made the background for the next part of the panel.

This produced such a lovely effect that I scanned the silk into a paint program and added a little more colour with the paintbrush tool. This design proved most useful and was incorporated in several ways, as you can see.

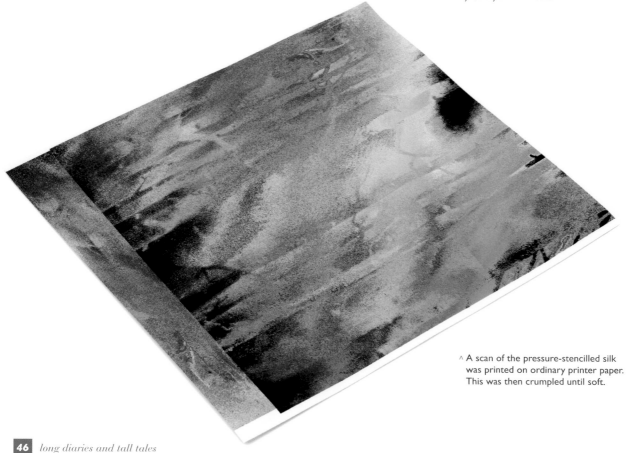

^ A scan of the pressure-stencilled silk
was printed on ordinary printer paper.
This was then crumpled until soft.

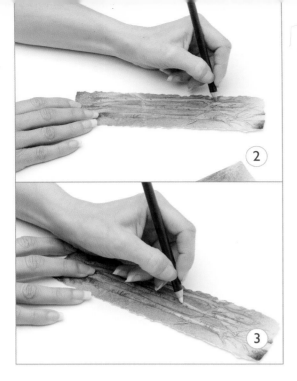

f. Crumpled paper with drawing pencils

1. A scan of the pressure-stencilled silk was printed on ordinary printer paper. This was then crumpled until soft.

2. When soft and floppy, it was torn into strips and the shapes of the trees were enhanced with Coloursoft drawing pencils using soft greys and browns, with a darker brown for the edges of the trunk.

3. The centres of the trunks were highlighted with a white Coloursoft pencil.

4. The edges of the strips were darkened with a drawing pen and the final step was a coat of acrylic wax to protect the paper. It was stuck to craft Vilene using the same glue-stick method as the birch tree cards on page 36, forming raised areas for the trunks.

5. When the glue was dry, each strip was hand stitched with toning thread. Running and back stitches along the trunks held the paper firmly to the base. A coat of acrylic wax was applied and, when this was dry, the finished strips were stitched on top of the pressure-stencilled silk from (e).

> Crumpled paper trees with some stitching.

g. White Sand Texture Gel

I was introduced to this idea by my friend Samantha Packer and it's very simple and effective. I use Pebeo White Sand Texture Gel but any of the heavy texture products should work. This is what you do:

1. Paint a piece of craft Vilene, a little larger than your stencil, with vibrant colour. I use Adirondack Spray paints but a strong mix of Brusho will do the trick. Mix two or three colours by spraying in separate areas and allowing them to merge. Don't be mean with the paint.

2. Lay the stencil over the painted Vilene and use a palette knife to spread the gel over the top.

3. Leave to dry and watch as the colour from the background wicks up into the pale gel.

4. The colours take time to develop – sometimes a couple of days. They will then become very vibrant and the joy of it is that the coating will always relate well to its background.

5. A little hand stitching added to the non-stencilled areas adds to the effect – simple running stitch is good.

Two small panels were made like this. One was set into the backing by cutting a hole, smaller than the inset, and stitching it around the edges to the back of the fabric. The other, larger, piece was applied on top of the backing.

h. Evolon

Evolon is a soft, suede-like fabric which can be painted or printed. It tends to make designs paler and rather washed out, which can be just what you need. If you want vibrant colours, give it a coat of inkAID, as described in the last section (see page 37). You can also splash it with water when freshly printed and, depending on your printer ink, this results in some areas losing all definition – good for fading Mythagos. When the ink had quite dried, the tree shapes were enhanced with free machine stitching.

< White Sand Texture Gel applied over a stencil. The Vilene background has been heavily painted so that the colour is pulled up into the gel.

∧ Paper and inkAID map from the base of the panel.

i. InkAID and scrim

Just the bottom to go now and for this I found our hero a map showing the location of Peace Island. This came from a photograph from a book of very old maps in a museum (with permission). I printed it and then had fun inking in more serpents. It was then scanned back into the paint program. Scrim was stuck to a heavy paper and inkAID applied over the top. When dry, the design was printed on this paper and given a light rubbing of gold metallic wax. This formed the bottom of the panel.

Finally the Maiden, the Peace Seeker and the Wise Woman were all stitched in place.

Extension technique

Just as I had hoped, the panel provided inspiration for the next part of the story. The top of the panel reminded me of a Book of Hours and that seemed a good format to use for two smaller versions of the original panel. I worked on the usual Vilene for a backing and retained the silk-printed semi-circle at the top to provide continuity. The same techniques and colours linked the new pieces to the first panels although the design differed slightly.

Two new characters appeared:

- Evil Rameses, who guarded Peace Island and caused the sea to bubble up and swallow all who tried to cross the Channel of Peace
- the Peace Horse who carried the Peace Seeker over the boiling sea while the Wood Warriors held the evil one in an enchantment.

In the final panel, yet to be completed, peace triumphs as Rameses joins the peace movement and grows flowers all over his skull. I do think that we need to know the techniques and stories behind these new characters.

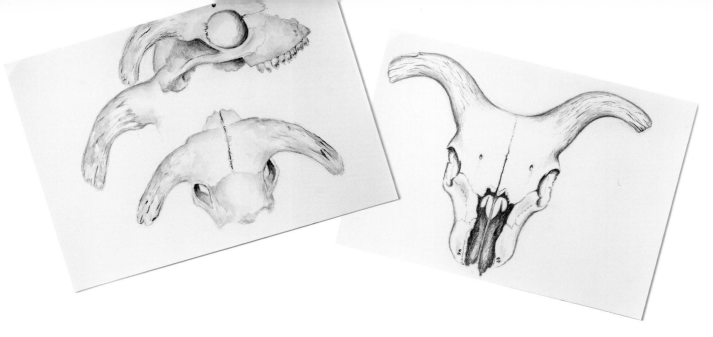

The story of Evil Rameses

Nikki Jones' ram's skull certainly fitted as a character in this tall tale and I took the liberty of turning it into a character in my story. The artwork was photographed for the Evil Rameses card, and Nikki's stitched piece for his more benevolent aspects. I asked her about the creation of the work and this is what she told me.

'I was inspired by Georgia O'Keeffe's, *Cow's Skull with Calico Roses*, and wanted to see if there was a way to explore this in fabric.

'I wanted the final piece to be very fine and delicate, the very opposite of the skull. Working with Nina Humphreys a few years ago, we

had experimented with wrapped stones, using watered-down PVA glue and slivers of hand-dyed scrim. The scrim layers were then cut off and the seams glue-gunned together. Embroidered slips were added to it to hide the glue-gun line. It seemed that this method could be adapted to the "found" skull. I wrapped it in clingfilm and then, as a sample, covered the skull in PVA-soaked scrim with minimal layers. I wanted to achieve an almost transparent effect with the stitching then appearing to float. The slips were created using a variety of hand stitches on the scrim, net and lace.

Once I was happy with the sample, I then worked the skull again using hand-dyed scrim and a suitable colour scheme.'

∧ Nikki Jones' artwork for the skull is shown above and below.

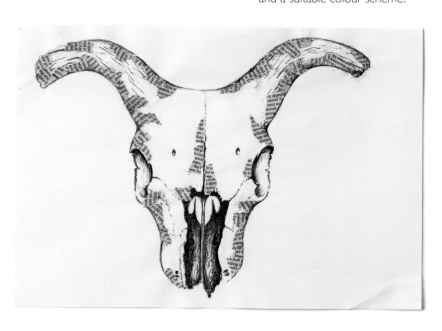

> Scrim layers were formed over the skull and stiffened with PVA. This was then stitched to give soft flowery effects.

< Nikki's initial experiment at moulding fabric, using the skull as a base.

∧ My original drawing of the Peace Horse plus a detail of the stitched version.

Saved by the Peace Horse

The Peace Horse evolved from a drawing which has been in my file for a long time, waiting to be used. For his role in the story, I showed him emerging magically from the forest, ready to take our hero safely to Peace Island and save the world. The design was printed on Evolon with stitched scrim applied. This was stuck firmly to printer paper and run through the printer.

So now you know the plot and have met all the characters, you can read more of the story on the next two pages.

> The drawing was scanned and pasted over a stencilled tree background. It was printed on Evolon previously coated with inkAID.

Putting it together

The panel was worked on Vilene as before with the cards added on top of the background. A metal boss adds focus to the top of the panel.

A Book of Hours was the inspiration for the format of this piece. It's a good device for story-telling as it features a prominent picture and lettering. For the traditional large capital letter, I found that Pebeo Prisme and a twinchie was an ideal combination.

This episode of the Peace Story shows the Peace Horse rising from the forest and preparing to take our heroes across the stormy water to Peace Island. There they will overcome the evil and bring down the baddie. The characters are shown as tarot-type cards. We have the Peace-seeker, the Maiden, the Wise Woman and Rameses, in his not so evil form.

Conclusion

The story has been told and my book of long diaries and tall tales has also reached an end. I do hope that you have enjoyed it and that you will be making your own versions. Whether it's a special holiday journal or a tall tale for a small person, make sure that you have fun.

These are the components of the next panel which will tell the story of the events on Peace Island. Here we see how the evil Rameses turned into Flowery Rameses after casting his eyes on the Peace Horse. All our 'baddies' become 'goodies' at this point and peace is restored to the world.

The textile will be made in the same way as the panel. The pictorial element will show how Nikki Jones' skull drawing, scanned into a paint program, morphed into a flowery Rameses form. All these elements will be constructed as in the panel on p53.

The Treasure Keeper

We have discussed the idea of the diary and story panels acting as a springboard for extension techniques. The idea of a 'Treasure Keeper' came about when our hero reached his destination and found not only peace but a magical talisman to ensure that the peace lasted. This little keeper, which is 15 cm (6 in) tall, was made from triangles of craft Vilene which were lightly wired to hold their contents safely. The contents are indeed treasures: two beaded beads made for me by the late Val Campbell-Harding. The painted exterior was decorated by hand stitching and couching techniques. If you have access to Facebook and would like to be 'my friend', you will find a video of this couching technique on my Facebook page.

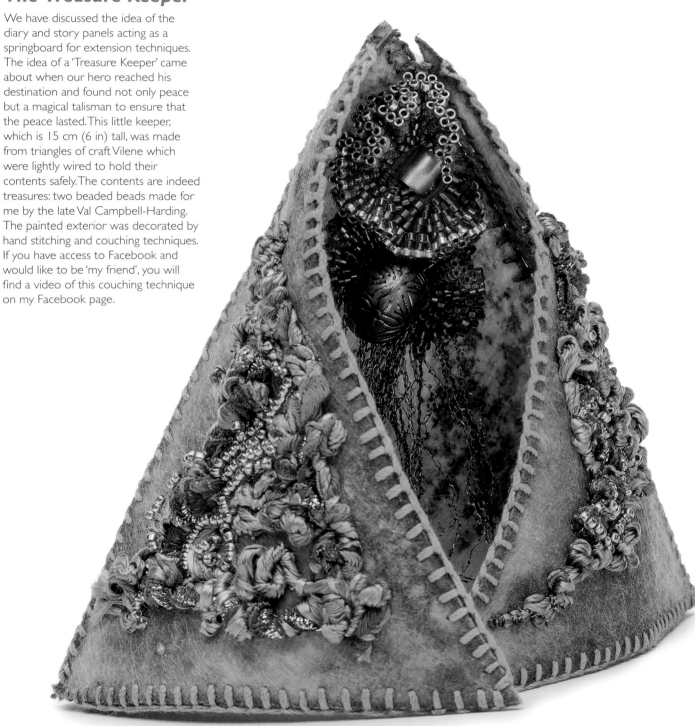